# BRILLIANT
# TRACES

## BY CINDY LOU JOHNSON

★

★

DRAMATISTS
PLAY SERVICE
INC.

BRILLIANT TRACES
Copyright © 1989, Cindy Lou Johnson

All Rights Reserved

2

# INDIVIDUATION

## AVAH PEVLOR JOHNSON

If I must be wrung through the paradox,
   — broken into wholeness,
wring me around the moon;
pelt me with particles from the dark side.

Fling me into space;
     hide me in a black hole.

Let me dance with devils on dead stars.
Let my scars leave brilliant traces,

for my highborn soul seeks its hell —
     in high places.

BRILLIANT TRACES was first presented by the Circle Repertory Company at the Cherry Lane Theatre, in New York City, on February 5, 1989. It was directed by Terry Kinney; the sets were by John Lee Beatty; the costume design was by Laura Crow; the lighting was by Dennis Parichy; the sound design was by Chuck London/Stewart Werner; and the production stage manager was Fred Reinglas. The cast, in order of appearance, was as follows:

HENRY HARRY. . . . . . . . . . . . . . . . . . . Kevin Anderson
ROSANNAH DELUCE. . . . . . . . . . . . . . . . Joan Cusack

# BRILLIANT TRACES

*A pool of moonlight falls into the empty room. There is a
pounding at the door.*

ROSANNAH. (*Off.*) Anybody there? If anybody's there, let
me in! I'm a person in serious trouble. (*Banging and kicking
continue. Then, suddenly, with one loud crash, the door bangs
open and an exhausted, freezing woman, Rosannah DeLuce,
bursts in. She is wearing a wedding gown and veil. Also silver
satin slippers. She is wet and cold to the bone. Her satin and lace
cling to her and droop like a living thing that has died on her skin.
The wind outside is howling. She struggles to close the door. Then
she turns, and what had formerly appeared to be nothing more
than a pile of blankets on the bed, has suddenly transmogrified
into a shrouded figure, standing. The lights brighten and ex-
pand. She backs up, truly frightened and on guard.*) Why didn't
you answer the door? (*She gets no response from the blanketed
form and continues with more courage.*) I could've frozen to
death! My death would've been on your hands, had that been
the case. It's something like two hundred degrees below out
there with the windchill, and I've been walking for over an
hour. My car died. DEAD. I left it somewhere. I don't even
know where. By now I'm sure it's totally buried in the snow
—out there — somewhere. (*Noticing the bottle of whiskey and a
glass on the table.*) Do you mind if I have a drink? (*She helps
herself to some whiskey. The figure remains frozen solid.*) I'm
nearly frozen and also may already be suffering from frost-
bite of the extremities, like my toes for example and my
fingers, though I was able to keep my fingers from falling off
by sticking them in my armpits. I saw that on a TV movie. A
man was in a skiing accident, immobilized, and they were
taking forever to get a stretcher brought down or something, so he asked this beautiful nurse, who *conveniently* happened to be there, couldn't she *do* something, because he was
freezing unto death, and so she stuck his hands in his armpits.
That's how she saved him! He fell in love with her then and
there, and married her later in the show. This is always the
story of my life — I have to play all the roles. I have to be the
one in trouble and be the nurse too — sticking my own

7

fingers into my own armpits, saving myself. All my life it's been like that. But the problem is, you can't stick your feet anywhere — not if you want to keep walking. (*Pouring more whiskey.*) Do you mind terribly much if I just — (*She downs the whiskey, puts the glass down, and takes in the entire room.*) So this is Alaska! (*She collapses into the chair and lets her shoes slip off her feet. She picks up a foot and examines it disconsolately.*) Oh my Lord. It is harder to believe than I can say that I am even so much as alive. (*Rubbing her feet.*) Oh! Oh! (*With relief as she massages them.*) Ooooooooooh. . . . When the car died, I could just *hear* the wind. I could just *hear* it, and the snow was falling so fast that the windshield was just covered instantly. Instantly! And it was getting colder in there by the second — I said, "Rosannah, this is it for you." I mean I knew if I stayed in that car, I'd fall asleep and freeze and die, and I knew if I got out of the car, in that wind and all that, I'd fall down and freeze and die. Freezing and dying was up there in the forefront of my brain of things to consider. But I thought — getting out — you know — walking — there's a chance anyway — I mean a slim chance, but a chance, so I got out. Interesting thing about being on the verge of death — you don't think about the good points or bad points of life — you just think LIVE! Let there be someone. A light. Some warmth. That's all I thought. And then I saw your light. And here I am. (*She pours more whiskey and then turns reassuringly to the form.*) I'll pay for this. (*She swallows.*) You see — I have been on the road for days. Days and days. This is the truth I'm telling you. I don't even know when I got in my car or where I've been. All I know is every five hours — gas. That's been my system. Gas — pee — eat a candy bar — drink a Coke. Go! Like the engine's inside me and not the car. Just like that. (*She finishes the whiskey and is distracted by a bag of pretzels on the counter. She gets up and goes to get them.*) Could I possibly eat these pretzels, because it's just about candy bar time for me and I do not see any candy bars. Anyway it's best I lay off sugar. I am getting the veritable sugar shakes. I have, in fact, had nothing to eat but sugar in quite some number of days. It's cheap energy, but sooner or later, in the case of sugar, you got to pay the piper as I am doing now. See my hands tremble? (*She shows him.*) That's a Mars Bars tremble.

Plus I have not slept in several days — not that I didn't try, but I was *A-WAKE*, with a capital W — like *my* wake is what it was like. The hours passed — the road kind of bleared behind me, so I am tired, and hungry, and the truth of the matter — very dirty. Well, let's call a spade a spade. I'm filthy. I have sweat too much, and this dress is a very close fit in the best of circumstances. Well, the absolute truth of the matter is, I am in pain. I am in terrible pain. That is the only reason I would drink this so hard and fast. It's not my muscles — but it's inside my muscles — you know? Like in my genes. My DNA. Yes, I think that must be it. My DNA . . . or my RNA, I'm not sure. (*Suddenly a moan issues from her, almost uncontrollably. She stops it as soon as she can. Then, apologizing.*) Excuse me. It's nothing really — Mmmmmmmph — just terrible pain in my DNA. That's all . . . (*Getting very dizzy.*) I'm dreadfully sorry. I'm more sorry than I can say, but . . . (*She crumples in a heap on the floor, her dress billowing up around her, swallowing her whole. The blanketed form moves forward, examines her, and then backs away. Finally it drops the blankets and becomes a man, HENRY HARRY. He stands in front of her and then, very slowly, and very gently, picks her up and holds her in his arms. She moans softly. He carries her over to his cot and lays her down. He looks at her for several moments. Then, slowly, he unbuttons her dress and removes it. He takes off her veil, stockings, slip, and jewelry — everything down to her underwear and camisole, both white. Then he gets a bowl of warm water and a cloth. He brings them over and carefully washes and dries her. Next, he gets a quilt and covers her gently. He backs away slightly, and examines her. She is dead asleep. He turns and walks all the way across the room. He picks up one of her shoes and sinks into a chair, holding the shoe tight. Finally, he collapses, letting the shoe fall. Lights dim back to a pool of moonlight. He puts his head in his hands. He sobs. Lights out. Lights up dimly to nighttime. Rosannah rises, though she doesn't seem fully awake.*) I am . . . I am . . . I am . . . (*Henry Harry, from the floor across the room where he is asleep, rises and looks over to her. She faces out, unaware of him, unaware she's even talking.*) I am the prettiest girl you have ever seen. (*Henry Harry looks at her warily but she continues to look out, almost as if she is searching, but for something*

9

*in her dreaming vision and not in the room. Lights out. Lights up to Henry Harry in a pool of moonlight. He is sitting in a chair next to where Rosannah continues to sleep. His arms are folded and he rocks his body back and forth, slowly, ceaselessly and silently, never taking his eyes off her as the lights fade to black. Lights up to daytime. Rosannah is asleep. Henry Harry is stirring soup at the stove. Rosannah suddenly wakes up, exhaling a light moan as she does. Henry Harry turns, looking at her. She sits up, takes in the room, and then, finally, her eyes land on him. She is confused.)*

HENRY HARRY. Hi.
ROSANNAH. *(Very still.)* Hi.
HENRY HARRY. You're awake.
ROSANNAH. Yes.
HENRY HARRY. You slept a long time.
ROSANNAH. How long?
HENRY HARRY. A couple of days.
ROSANNAH. A couple of days?!
HENRY HARRY. Yes.
ROSANNAH. Oh my God.
HENRY HARRY. You were tired.
ROSANNAH. Oh my God! *(She looks at the bed.)* I've been in this bed a couple of days?
HENRY HARRY. Yes.
ROSANNAH. I arrived here two days ago?
HENRY HARRY. Yes.
ROSANNAH. Were you here?
HENRY HARRY. Yes. *(Rosannah pulls the covers back, about to get out of bed. She sees she's undressed, and quickly covers herself a bit awkwardly. Henry Harry is facing her directly and cannot avoid seeing this. After a pause.)* There are some clothes for you. *(He motions to a stack of neatly folded clothes on a stool next to the bed. There are pants, a shirt, socks and shoes.)* I thought you might need some clothes.
ROSANNAH. Oh. *(She looks at the pile of clothes, and then back to Henry Harry. He sees this, and quickly turns away.)*
HENRY HARRY. I made some soup. Let me see if it's still hot. *(He goes to the stove to check the soup. Rosannah gets up. She sees his back is to her. She gets out of bed, putting on the shirt and pants. While she is doing this, he sneaks a look over to see if she's*

10

*dressing. Seeing that she is, he turns back to give her privacy. She doesn't see this action.*) Yeah it is. It's hot. (*Tasting it.*) Mmmmmm. It always tastes better the second day. Actually I made it yesterday, but you didn't wake up, so now it's the second day. It's better. (*He steals a look again. She's buttoning the shirt and looks up to see him watching her.*)

ROSANNAH. Um. Thank you. (*Henry Harry starts to look away but Rosannah continues.*) These are warm. Thank you.

HENRY HARRY. You're welcome.

ROSANNAH. (*Beat.*) I'm just wondering. I mean . . . when I came in here — when I arrived . . . was I wearing? . . . I mean where are my clothes?

HENRY HARRY. Your *gown*?

ROSANNAH. Yes.

HENRY HARRY. I hung it up.

ROSANNAH. And my shoes?

HENRY HARRY. Those slippers?

ROSANNAH. Yes.

HENRY HARRY. I . . . well, I couldn't quite figure out what to do with them. I put them in the oven, you know, to kind of dry them out . . . and then . . . accidentally, I turned it up when I was making dinner — I mean, I forgot. So they um. . . . they got cooked.

ROSANNAH. Cooked?

HENRY HARRY. Yeah. Pretty much.

ROSANNAH. Oh.

HENRY HARRY. I'm sorry.

ROSANNAH. (*Despondent.*) Oh . . . (*Trying to straighten up.*) No. That's alright.

HENRY HARRY. They weren't in great condition anyhow.

ROSANNAH. No, I'm sure they weren't.

HENRY HARRY. And they weren't exactly the kind of shoes you could . . .

ROSANNAH. What?

HENRY HARRY. Well, I mean, they were a very specific type shoe.

ROSANNAH. Oh.

HENRY HARRY. I mean they weren't the kind of shoe you could actually have *worn* anywhere.

ROSANNAH. Oh.

11

HENRY HARRY. I mean — certainly not *here*.

ROSANNAH. No.

HENRY HARRY. They looked like they were made out of *paper*.

ROSANNAH. They were satin.

HENRY HARRY. Oh.

ROSANNAH. With lace edges.

HENRY HARRY. Oh. Well . . .

ROSANNAH. They cost a hundred and twenty-five dollars.

HENRY HARRY. A hundred and twenty-five dollars!

ROSANNAH. Yes.

HENRY HARRY. Jesus!

ROSANNAH. It doesn't matter.

HENRY HARRY. Jesus Christ!

ROSANNAH. It's ok.

HENRY HARRY. But they were . . . they were only this big. (*He gesticulates the size of a tiny shoe.*)

ROSANNAH. Well, they were for my *wedding*.

HENRY HARRY. Oh. I'm really sorry I cooked them.

ROSANNAH. It's alright. (*There is a brief awkward silence.*)

HENRY HARRY. (*Putting a spoon, bread, and butter etc. on the table.*) Why don't you eat?

ROSANNAH. Oh ok. (*She doesn't move. Instead she stares at Henry Harry.*)

HENRY HARRY. (*Pointing to the table.*) Over here.

ROSANNAH. (*Still staring.*) Have we met?

HENRY HARRY. When?

ROSANNAH. Earlier.

HENRY HARRY. Well, no. I mean the other night we . . . we didn't exactly meet but . . .

ROSANNAH. What?

HENRY HARRY. Well, you *arrived*.

ROSANNAH. (*Re-stating this, trying to get information.*) I arrived.

HENRY HARRY. Yes, and then, shortly thereafter, you . . . well you went to sleep . . . suddenly.

ROSANNAH. I went to sleep? I just lay down and went to sleep?

HENRY HARRY. Yes. Well, no. You kind of . . . fainted.

ROSANNAH. Fainted?

HENRY HARRY. Unhunh. I think the soup's cooled off now. Why don't you try it?

ROSANNAH. I don't remember fainting.

HENRY HARRY. I do. I remember.

ROSANNAH. I just fell down onto the floor?

HENRY HARRY. You sort of sank. Very gently.

ROSANNAH. (*Trying to visualize this.*) Oh. I sank. (*Beat.*) Then how did I . . . ? (*Looking at the bed.*) I mean, I woke up in that bed.

HENRY HARRY. Oh. Well, I put you there. (*Rosannah looks up at him startled.*) I mean you were on the floor. So I put you there.

ROSANNAH. Oh.

HENRY HARRY. That's all.

ROSANNAH. Oh . . . and then I just slept like that — in that bed — for two days? Not moving?

HENRY HARRY. Yes. (*Pauses.*) Well, one time — I think it was the first night — you sort of rose up.

ROSANNAH. I rose up?

HENRY HARRY. Yes. I mean in the bed. You kind of rose up, but I don't really think you were awake. I think you were dreaming.

ROSANNAH. I just rose, dreaming?

HENRY HARRY. Yes.

ROSANNAH. I just . . . what do you mean, I "rose up"?

HENRY HARRY. Well, you sat up very slowly and you sort of spoke. But you didn't seem conscious. It was like you were dreaming. You didn't seem awake at all.

ROSANNAH. What did I say?

HENRY HARRY. You just . . . I don't know . . . you were just . . . you know — dreaming. Mumbling. You were probably just talking in your sleep. Are you hungry? You must be starving.

ROSANNAH. Could you understand anything I said?

HENRY HARRY. When?

ROSANNAH. When I rose up and spoke. Could you understand anything I said?

HENRY HARRY. (*Reluctantly.*) Unhunh.

ROSANNAH. What was it? What did I say?

HENRY HARRY. Well, you said . . . (*He stops for a mo-*

*ment, then looks directly at Rosannah.*) you said you were the prettiest girl I'd ever seen. (*Rosannah is startled. She stares at Henry Harry for a moment, and then looks away.*)

ROSANNAH. Oh . . . well . . . that's strange. That's very odd.

HENRY HARRY. Why don't you sit down? (*Rosannah doesn't move.*) Here. Really. Why don't you sit — (*Seeing Rosannah is too dazed and lost to move, Henry Harry finally takes her to the chair. He seats her.*) Here. I think if you just sit here and have some soup. (*He moves the bowl in front of her. She smiles weakly, but then flies back into herself, disturbed. She glances briefly at the bowl but takes no action. Finally he takes her spoon.*) Here. (*Feeding her.*) There. (*He feeds her one spoonful after the next. She takes three or four bites slowly, in this way, then jumps up, abruptly, grabbing the spoon from his hand.*)

ROSANNAH. What are you doing?

HENRY HARRY. What?

ROSANNAH. I can feed myself! I don't need anybody to feed me. Who do you think I am? Somebody who *needs* someone to feed her?

HENRY HARRY. (*Backing up.*) No . . . I . . . No. (*Rosannah puts the spoon down. She sits back down.*)

ROSANNAH. (*Embarrassed by the outburst.*) Excuse me.

HENRY HARRY. That's alright.

ROSANNAH. I'm terribly sorry. I don't know what's wrong with me. (*Beat.*) I don't quite know. (*She eats. Henry Harry watches.*)

HENRY HARRY. (*After a pause.*) I'm really *very* sorry I cooked your shoes.

ROSANNAH. Oh . . . well . . . anyway . . .

HENRY HARRY. I would have been more careful if I'd realized their value.

ROSANNAH. Yes . . . no, that's alright. The soup's good.

HENRY HARRY. Oh.

ROSANNAH. Very tasty. (*She jumps up abruptly.*) I'd better go.

HENRY HARRY. What?

ROSANNAH. Do you know exactly where I am?

HENRY HARRY. What do you mean?

ROSANNAH. (*Vaguely.*) I have to call the people.

HENRY HARRY. What people?

ROSANNAH. Those men who fix things. . . . you know . . . because my car . . . I'm very dizzy.

HENRY HARRY. Here. Sit down. (*He sits her down.*) You don't have much color. I think you really need to eat. I mean, I really think you need to eat *a lot!*

ROSANNAH. No. I'd better — (*She almost tries to stand back up.*)

HENRY HARRY. I think you're depleted. You look depleted.

ROSANNAH. (*Panicked.*) Where am I? What is this place?

HENRY HARRY. *Here?*

ROSANNAH. Yes.

HENRY HARRY. This is my home.

ROSANNAH. Oh. (*She glances around.*) It's very nice.

HENRY HARRY. Thank you. Here. (*Handing her a spoon.*) I think you're weaker than you realize.

ROSANNAH. No. I realize I'm weak. I'm fully aware of it. I'm a very weak person.

HENRY HARRY. I wasn't saying you were a weak person. I'm sure you're not a weak person. I'm sure you're just —

ROSANNAH. It's because I'm so limited. I'm terribly limited.

HENRY HARRY. What?

ROSANNAH. I am. I wish I weren't. I wish I were — *expansive* — you know. But I'm not. I'm limited. Terribly, terribly limited.

HENRY HARRY. I think you need some more soup.

ROSANNAH. And I don't know how I got this way. Somehow my perspective has been narrowed — I think I am living in the clutches of a very narrow perspective. And I don't think that's fair. I think if you're in the clutches of a very narrow perspective, you shouldn't *know* about it. You'd be satisfied, but *knowing*, being fully aware — I mean —

HENRY HARRY. (*Handing her the spoon again.*) I think you're just hungry.

ROSANNAH. (*Stopping and focusing on him.*) Oh. (*She looks down into her bowl. She eats. She eats it all.*) There. I ate it all. I feel better. Thank you.

HENRY HARRY. You're welcome.

ROSANNAH. I feel — nourished.

HENRY HARRY. Good.

ROSANNAH. I was just a bit confused back there. For good reason. I've been traveling a long time, and then there was that storm and all, and then sleeping for two days. You can imagine that would confuse anyone. Don't you think?

HENRY HARRY. Yes I do. I think it would. Why don't you eat your bread?

ROSANNAH. What?

HENRY HARRY. (*Buttering it.*) Here. There. It's all buttered. (*Rosannah stops, surprised.*) I'm sorry. I didn't mean to butter it. I am sure you can butter your own bread. I am sure you're the kind of person who can butter her own bread. Here's another piece. (*He slices another piece.*) You butter it. This one's for me. (*He takes a bite of the one he's buttered.*) That's yours. (*He points to the other one.*)

ROSANNAH. No, thank you.

HENRY HARRY. It's really good bread.

ROSANNAH. I'm pretty full.

HENRY HARRY. Please (*Beat.*) I made it myself. You could just try it.

ROSANNAH. (*Pauses and then takes a bite.*) It's good.

HENRY HARRY. Don't you want some butter on it?

ROSANNAH. (*Examining him.*) You're the kind of person who takes care of people, aren't you?

HENRY HARRY. What?

ROSANNAH. I see that you're the kind of person who takes care of people — watches out for them. Feels responsible.

HENRY HARRY. No. I'm not. I don't.

ROSANNAH. Well, you certainly come across as the kind of person who —

HENRY HARRY. (*Cutting her off.*) I'm not that kind of person.

ROSANNAH. Oh. (*Eating her bread.*) Do you live here alone?

HENRY HARRY. Yes.

ROSANNAH. No family? No —

HENRY HARRY. (*Cutting her off.*) You done?

ROSANNAH. Yes. (*He roughly clears the table. Rosannah watches him for several moments.*) My name's Rosannah DeLuce.

16

HENRY HARRY. (*Not turning around.*) Henry Harry.
ROSANNAH. What?
HENRY HARRY. I'm Henry Harry.
ROSANNAH. Oh. (*Beat.*) You've been very kind . . . I mean, thank you for —
HENRY HARRY. (*Cutting her off.*) You were almost frozen to death. I didn't do anything you wouldn't do for a sick dog.
ROSANNAH. Oh.
HENRY HARRY. Someone comes banging into your home, you don't have to be any particular kind of person to *feed* them.
ROSANNAH. No I wasn't implying —
HENRY HARRY. You'd have to be pretty far gone if you didn't even *feed* them.
ROSANNAH. That's true. I was just making an observation — I mean it just crossed my mind that —
HENRY HARRY. Any one human being on this earth would feed another if he was sitting right in front of him and so hungry he couldn't even think straight.
ROSANNAH. (*Gently but firmly.*) I can think straight. I thought we had established that I was feeling a little disoriented, like any *normal* human being would if they'd been driving for many, many days and then been sleeping for two. I can think very straight. (*She pauses, but Henry Harry does not respond.*) Yes . . . well I guess I'd better see about my car. (*She heads to the door.*)
HENRY HARRY. (*Turning.*) Where are you going?
ROSANNAH. I'm going to see about my car.
HENRY HARRY. It's still snowing like crazy out there.
ROSANNAH. Well, I'll just see why it died.
HENRY HARRY. See why it died? You won't even see your car.
ROSANNAH. I'll do my best. (*She turns back to the door.*)
HENRY HARRY. Sit down.
ROSANNAH. (*Startled.*) What?
HENRY HARRY. SIT BACK DOWN!
ROSANNAH. Excuse me, but if I want to go look at my car —
HENRY HARRY. You walk ten feet out there everything'll just look white and you'll be lost and frozen.

ROSANNAH. I can find my way to my car. (*She opens the door. Suddenly, and with force, Henry Harry is in front of her. He slams the door closed.*) What are you doing?

HENRY HARRY. Didn't you *hear* me?

ROSANNAH. You're not going to let me *out?*

HENRY HARRY. You'll freeze to death!

ROSANNAH. I will not! (*She grabs the door. He grabs her arm.*) OW! Let go!

HENRY HARRY. You want me to just let you go out there and freeze to death?

ROSANNAH. Let go!

HENRY HARRY. No.

ROSANNAH. (*Struggling.*) Let me go!

HENRY HARRY. No! (*Rosannah suddenly punches him. He is taken off guard and falls. She runs to the door. He gets up and catches her. They struggle. Finally he gets her pinned against the wall.*) I'm not going to let you go out there. For Christ's sake. I *washed* you! (*Rosannah is stunned. Henry Harry lets her go. He is badly shaken.*) I'm sorry. (*Rosannah sees how broken up he is. She examines him from a distance. He does not see this.*)

ROSANNAH. I can look at my car later. (*Henry Harry nods, beaten. After a pause.*) Do you have any tea?

HENRY HARRY. What?

ROSANNAH. I could make us some tea. I feel like I could really use some tea right now. How about you?

HENRY HARRY. It's on the shelf.

ROSANNAH. Why don't you sit down?

HENRY HARRY. Yeah. (*He doesn't move.*)

ROSANNAH. Why don't you sit here? (*Henry Harry looks up vaguely. Then he sits where Rosannah is holding out the chair. Rosannah stands next to him, looking for a moment, then withdraws to the stove.*) I'll just use this pot. Is this pot alright? (*Henry Harry is oblivious.*) I'll just use this pot. (*She fills it with water and puts it on the stove. She watches it.*) It'll just take a minute.

HENRY HARRY. It's none of my business *what* you do.

ROSANNAH. What?

HENRY HARRY. If you want to go find your car, it's certainly none of my business. Go ahead!

ROSANNAH. That's ok.
HENRY HARRY. There's the door.
ROSANNAH. No, I'd rather not.
HENRY HARRY. You can wear my coat if you want. I don't care.
ROSANNAH. I'm making tea right now. (*Henry Harry turns back around, very conflicted.*)
HENRY HARRY. I didn't mean to cook your shoes.
ROSANNAH. It's really alright.
HENRY HARRY. By the time you'd walked through the field with them and everything, they were pretty ruined already.
ROSANNAH. Yeah. I know.
HENRY HARRY. I mean they were discolored and sort of misshapen.
ROSANNAH. Yeah.
HENRY HARRY. I don't think they were still worth a hundred and twenty-five dollars by the time I cooked them.
ROSANNAH. I'm sure they weren't even worth ten cents.
HENRY HARRY. I don't know why I put them in the oven. I just didn't know what to *do* with them. I mean there they were, all crumply and papery or satiny or whatever. They were just lying there, under the table — you took them off before you . . . you know . . . you went down, so they were kind of lying there where they'd fallen off your feet.
ROSANNAH. Yeah.
HENRY HARRY. One was upright, but the other was sideways.
ROSANNAH. Oh.
HENRY HARRY. The toe was sort of pointed off that way. (*He points.*) I mean I just don't normally have things like that lying around here. I usually don't have anything lying around here that I don't personally *put* wherever it's lying around.
ROSANNAH. Oh.
HENRY HARRY. So, it threw me. That's all. So I stuck them in the oven so I wouldn't have to be staring at them, and *then*, because I usually don't have silver slippers in my oven, I turned it on without really thinking about it.
ROSANNAH. Yeah.

19

HENRY HARRY. That's the whole story.

ROSANNAH. The truth of the matter is, they're pretty useless shoes. Either you're getting married and you wear them, or you're not and you don't so . . . (*Smelling the package of tea.*) What kind of tea is this?

HENRY HARRY. Gung Bang.

ROSANNAH. Gung BANG?

HENRY HARRY. It's Chinese.

ROSANNAH. Oh.

HENRY HARRY. It's alright. It clears your head.

ROSANNAH. Oh. Well. That's good. That'll come in handy. (*She puts tea in two mugs, puts in water and brings them to the table. Giving one to Henry Harry.*) Here.

HENRY HARRY. Thanks. (*She sits down. They are opposite each other, but Henry Harry is very distracted, not quite connecting with Rosannah.*) As soon as this storm is over, I'll fix your car.

ROSANNAH. Oh. I can call someone.

HENRY HARRY. It's ok. I can do it. I'm very handy. I'll fix it and you can get on to wherever it is you're going.

ROSANNAH. Oh. Alright. Thanks.

HENRY HARRY. I'd be out there right this minute, but it's just impossible conditions out there. There's a white out out there right now.

ROSANNAH. A white out?

HENRY HARRY. Yeah. That's what we get out here. White outs. The snow comes down — covers everything, and the sky's the same color as the ground and the air. You can't see clear to anything. It tricks your brain. You lose your balance. You almost start walking right into the air, but gravity attacks you and throws you down, but you don't know that. You may think you're flying up to heaven. You may think anything. Pretty soon you start to hallucinate. In the end you collapse and freeze and die of fear.

ROSANNAH. Oh.

HENRY HARRY. It happens all the time. Even to veterans of these parts.

ROSANNAH. It sound very dangerous.

HENRY HARRY. Dangerous? It's deadly. Believe me. I was out in one once. I thought I was a dead man. Everything went

20

white. I couldn't tell where to put my feet. I was stopped. I tried to move forward, but I had no confidence. No faith. I banged into my door. I thought it was the sky, but it had a handle. I pushed and fell inside — I was saved — I stood right over there, looking around my house thinking how everything has shape and form, but it could disappear in an instant. Right at this moment — right outside that door — it has all disappeared. If you have ever wondered what nothing looks like, go out there. Go out there! Go ahead.

ROSANNAH. No. (*She pauses.*) Thank you.

HENRY HARRY. Why not?

ROSANNAH. I don't care to.

HENRY HARRY. It's a sight to see.

ROSANNAH. That's alright.

HENRY HARRY. Everything transformed into nothing. You'd be transformed too. If you went out there, someone would look right at you and see nothing.

ROSANNAH. They would not!

HENRY HARRY. They would! They would! Every single particular detail about you would just disappear. You would be indistinguishable.

ROSANNAH. (*Suddenly exploding fiercely.*) I would not be indistinguishable! I am not indistinguishable! I am — (*She stops, suddenly finding herself raging, her arms in mid-air. She collects herself and then sits back down. After a pause, she continues, quieted down.*) I just don't feel like going out there. That's all.

HENRY HARRY. (*He watches her and then sips his tea.*) The tea's good. (*Rosannah doesn't respond.*) Nice and hot. Do you want some honey in yours?

ROSANNAH. No. Thank you.

HENRY HARRY. Or lemon or something?

ROSANNAH. No. This is fine. This is just what I needed.

HENRY HARRY. You do look a little better. I think you've got some color now. You were really pretty green earlier.

ROSANNAH. Well I'm fine now. I'm fine.

HENRY HARRY. Good. You look good. You look a lot better. (*Beat.*) So . . . ? (*He waits for a response.*)

ROSANNAH. What?

HENRY HARRY. Well, I was just wondering. I mean I have

21

been wondering, what exactly are you doing all the way out here?

ROSANNAH. Out here?

HENRY HARRY. Yeah. Out here. Way out here. There just aren't very many reasons for anyone to come way out here.

ROSANNAH. Oh. Well. My car died — you know.

HENRY HARRY. But you were already *here* when your car died. I mean you'd already gotten all the way out here *before* your car died.

ROSANNAH. Oh. Well . . . I just drove. I was just driving.

HENRY HARRY. Unhunh . . . What I'm saying is — this is not exactly on the way to anywhere. This is not exactly the crossroads. I guess what I'm saying is, there is nothing else out here, except me. So . . . I mean, did you get lost? (*Henry Harry waits, but gets no response.*) Did you lose your way?

ROSANNAH. No. I was really just trying to get some air in the car — a breeze — because it was very hot in there. It was a very hot day.

HENRY HARRY. *Hot?*

ROSANNAH. And then it seems like once I was driving, I couldn't stop. Even when I stopped, like for gas, it didn't really seem like I was stopping. It still felt like I was going, even when I was perfectly still, I was still going. I was flying. (*She pauses and then gravely and with fear.*) I don't think I'm altogether healthy.

HENRY HARRY. You don't?

ROSANNAH. No.

HENRY HARRY. Why not?

ROSANNAH. Because, although I was the one in the driver's seat all the way here — there was no one else — I was alone, *still*, I fear that was an illusion.

HENRY HARRY. An illusion?

ROSANNAH. I fear that I was, in fact, not in the driver's seat at all.

HENRY HARRY. Where were you?

ROSANNAH. I was above it.

HENRY HARRY. Above it?

ROSANNAH. *Well* above it. Not quite touching down. Just hovering.

HENRY HARRY. In the air? You were hovering in the air?

ROSANNAH. It doesn't sound very likely does it?

HENRY HARRY. Well . . .

ROSANNAH. I know it doesn't. But I am simply stating how it seemed to me at the time.

HENRY HARRY. Yeah . . . No, I understand.

ROSANNAH. I was almost grazing the seat, but not quite. So close, but not there. It became hard to tell which was the reality and which the illusion. It was just very hard to tell. It's been like that for days now. For example, I know I appear, at this moment, to be sitting here, in this chair, but I am not.

HENRY HARRY. (*Taking a glance at the chair.*) No?

ROSANNAH. No. Not from my point of view. From my point of view I am making no contact with this chair whatsoever. From my point of view I am still flying, as I was flying all the way here. I kept thinking—I am moving much faster than this car that carries me. I am traveling faster than sound or light. I am moving with such speed that I am truly in danger. I thought, surely I will fly right through this windshield. Surely I will hurtle into space. I thought that every minute. I don't know how I survived.

HENRY HARRY. Oh.

ROSANNAH. (*With fear.*) I don't sound altogether healthy do I?

HENRY HARRY. Well . . . no—I mean I'm sure you're fine . . . I—

ROSANNAH. I don't think so either. I mean to end up way out here. It's not very likely that anyone healthy would end up—(*She stops, noticing Henry Harry.*) I'm sure there are exceptions. (*Beat.*) I'm sure there are notable exceptions.

HENRY HARRY. I *live* here. (*Rosannah nods.*) This is my *house.*

ROSANNAH. Well, that's different.

HENRY HARRY. I didn't just *drive* here. I *live* here.

ROSANNAH. Yes. I see. That makes perfect sense. (*Beat.*) You live here. This is your house. (*Henry Harry nods.*)

HENRY HARRY. Yes. (*Rosannah nods.*)

ROSANNAH. Yes. So. How long have you lived here?

23

HENRY HARRY. A year.

ROSANNAH. A *year?*

HENRY HARRY. Yes.

ROSANNAH. Just *you?*

HENRY HARRY. What do you mean?

ROSANNAH. I mean just alone all the time?

HENRY HARRY. No. I'm not alone all the time. I have a job.

ROSANNAH. Oh.

HENRY HARRY. On an oil rig.

ROSANNAH. (*This sounds alright to her.*) Oh!

HENRY HARRY. I'm a cook.

ROSANNAH. Oh! I see! I see! You're a very good cook too!

HENRY HARRY. Thank you.

ROSANNAH. The bread and soup were delicious.

HENRY HARRY. Thank you.

ROSANNAH. I can't cook at all.

HENRY HARRY. No?

ROSANNAH. No. I mean. I can do it — I used to do it for my Dad — but I'm just not very creative at it. That's all.

HENRY HARRY. Oh.

ROSANNAH. Not like you.

HENRY HARRY. Oh well, I'm not —

ROSANNAH. (*Emphatically.*) Not to say my meals weren't edible. They were edible. (*Beat.*) More or less.

HENRY HARRY. Well, that's a start.

ROSANNAH. Yes.

HENRY HARRY. Yes. Well . . . so you used to live with your Dad?

ROSANNAH. Yes. I did. I used to. My mother left when I was young, so —

HENRY HARRY. Left?

ROSANNAH. Yes.

HENRY HARRY. Left you?

ROSANNAH. Yes. (*Beat.*) So it was just my Dad and me.

HENRY HARRY. Oh. Hunh. So, what's he do for a living — your Dad?

ROSANNAH. He's retired now. He used to repair refrigerators, but he forgot how.

HENRY HARRY. He forgot how?

ROSANNAH. Yes. He forgot small but very important details. That's what brains are like evidently. They just blink, blink, and then go dark.

HENRY HARRY. Blink blink? What do you mean — blink, blink?

ROSANNAH. Well. I found him one morning, crouching in front of his favorite armchair. He was poking it with the stick-end of the broom, like it might attack him. He said, "Rosannah, what is that thing?" I had to show him how you bend your knees and sit down, how you get comfortable. He was amazed. He said, "Imagine an inanimate object meeting you halfway like that."

HENRY HARRY. He got old?

ROSANNAH. Yes . . . yeah. So! Is your oil rig around here?

HENRY HARRY. What? Oh no. It's four hundred miles away.

ROSANNAH. Four hundred miles away?

HENRY HARRY. Yes.

ROSANNAH. Then why do you live here?

HENRY HARRY. We get off two weeks after every seven.

ROSANNAH. Oh. I see. So you're off now.

HENRY HARRY. Yes.

ROSANNAH. I guess you have to get off a lot, oil rigs being as isolated as they are.

HENRY HARRY. Yes. We do. The men start getting crazy or depressed or both after about six weeks.

ROSANNAH. That makes sense. I guess they need to get back to civilization.

HENRY HARRY. Yes.

ROSANNAH. (*After a pause in which she turns, taking in the room.*) So why do you come here?

HENRY HARRY. What do you mean?

ROSANNAH. Well, this is pretty remote.

HENRY HARRY. This is my home.

ROSANNAH. Yes, but what about people?

HENRY HARRY. What about them?

ROSANNAH. Don't you ever want to see people?

HENRY HARRY. No.

ROSANNAH. No? Never? No one?

HENRY HARRY. No. Never. No one. Never. No.

ROSANNAH. Oh . . . well . . . (*Beat.*) You must be just thrilled to pieces I blew in here.

HENRY HARRY. Look, it wasn't your fault you showed up here. I don't blame you.

ROSANNAH. (*Nodding nervously.*) Thank you.

HENRY HARRY. You were just driving. You drove here. That's how you have explained it, and that is how I understand it. Although, I must say, no one has ever accidentally driven here before.

ROSANNAH. I didn't come here accidentally.

HENRY HARRY. You came here on purpose?

ROSANNAH. No. I just . . . I came here by chance.

HENRY HARRY. By chance?

ROSANNAH. Well, I think I have explained, or tried to explain, that I am not quite clear about exactly what led me here. I was just in my car, and it was very hot in there, and I just thought I'd drive a few feet to get a little breeze on me, and then —

HENRY HARRY. What do you mean it was *hot*? You keep saying it was *hot*. I don't understand what you mean it was *hot*?

ROSANNAH. It was a hot day. The sun was beating down. It was hot! HOT! You know — HOT!

HENRY HARRY. The sun was beating down?

ROSANNAH. Yes.

HENRY HARRY. The sun hasn't beaten down around here in months.

ROSANNAH. Well, it was beating down when I started driving.

HENRY HARRY. (*Pauses.*) Exactly where were you when you started driving?

ROSANNAH. Arizona.

HENRY HARRY. ARIZONA!

ROSANNAH. Yes.

HENRY HARRY. You started driving in Arizona and drove non-stop, alone — "by chance" to Alaska?

ROSANNAH. This is where my car died.

HENRY HARRY. Jesus!

ROSANNAH. What?

26

HENRY HARRY. Jesus Christ!

ROSANNAH. What?

HENRY HARRY. What in God's name happened to you in Arizona that made you drive all the way to Alaska?

ROSANNAH. Nothing *happened* to me.

HENRY HARRY. Nothing *happened*? You were just at your wedding — in Arizona — walking up the aisle, and suddenly you thought — "I feel like taking a drive", and you zipped out of the church, hopped into your car and started *driving*, and kept *driving*, until your car *died* out *there*?

ROSANNAH. No. That's not what happened.

HENRY HARRY. What happened?

ROSANNAH. What do *you* care what happened? You only took me in because I reminded you of a sick dog —

HENRY HARRY. That's not what I meant.

ROSANNAH. It's what you said. And, by the way, if I may say so, I personally am slightly curious about a man who lives like a hermit, when he isn't on an oil rig — which already is just another form of living like a hermit if you ask me, and *then*, when someone finally does show up at his godforsaken door, he *only* takes them in because they remind him of a sick dog, and then he *cooks* their *shoes*!

HENRY HARRY. That was an accident! I'm just not used to total stranger's satin slippers being in *my* oven.

ROSANNAH. You put them there.

HENRY HARRY. Just because they were on the floor, looking . . .

ROSANNAH. What?

HENRY HARRY. Pathetic. (*Beat.*) They depressed the hell out of me. (*Rosannah is silent.*) I mean . . . they looked like they were make-believe . . . just all satiny and lacy . . . little silver slippers — like for a *doll* or something. Who even *has* shoes like that? And then, on top of it, they were all . . . *ruined*. And I couldn't fix them. I knew I couldn't. They were just tossed on the floor and one was up straight, and the other was pointing off, and they both were all droopy and crumpled and . . . WHAT THE HELL WAS I SUPPOSED TO DO WITH THEM? You just show up here. This is MY LIFE — and you just show up with ruined, make-believe doll shoes and what am I supposed to do? I put them

27

in the oven — I couldn't stand *looking* at them, and maybe I cooked them on purpose — I'm sorry! But I couldn't fix them. Don't you get it? (*Rosannah stares stunned. Henry Harry finally sits down, slowly. Rosannah gets up, trying to look efficient.*)

ROSANNAH. What I'll do — I'll call Triple A.

HENRY HARRY. Triple A?

ROSANNAH. And get somebody out here to fix my car.

HENRY HARRY. There isn't any Triple A out here.

ROSANNAH. Well, then a mechanic —

HENRY HARRY. Look, there is a white out out there. The phones are down — the roads are impassable. No one goes out in a white out.

ROSANNAH. Well, there must be a hotel or *some*thing.

HENRY HARRY. A *hotel*?!

ROSANNAH. Yes. I feel . . . I mean, I can plainly *see* that I'm in your way. (*Henry Harry looks up, startled.*) I just don't want to be in anybody's way. I'm sorry that my car died. I, perhaps, should not have driven it so hard, but somehow — I just lost track of time and —

HENRY HARRY. You just lost track of *time*? You mean you lost track of *weeks*.

ROSANNAH. I don't know.

HENRY HARRY. Well you must've been driving a couple of weeks.

ROSANNAH. I don't know.

HENRY HARRY. You don't *know*? You just have no idea? No idea at all?

ROSANNAH. No. I was just trying not to fly through the windshield. I was trying not to crash into space. I am still trying. Even as I am standing here. I am trying.

HENRY HARRY. (*Trying to get a grasp.*) You feel, right now, as we speak, that you might crash into space.

ROSANNAH. Yes.

HENRY HARRY. Right this minute, while you're standing there talking to me, you're hurtling forward?

ROSANNAH. Yes.

HENRY HARRY. Well, you're not. You're mistaken. You're just standing there.

ROSANNAH. It's hard to say.

28

HENRY HARRY. It's hard for *you* to say. It isn't hard for me to say. I can see you there. I can see you very plainly.
ROSANNAH. You see what you *can* see.
HENRY HARRY. I see what I *can* see?
ROSANNAH. I mean we, all of us, see what we *can* see. That's all.
HENRY HARRY. What else *could* we see?
ROSANNAH. I don't know, but sometimes we might get a hunch that there is something very important, vital, going on just beyond our peripheral vision. Sometimes we might get a hunch like that.
HENRY HARRY. I don't get those hunches.
ROSANNAH. You're lucky.
HENRY HARRY. No. My hunch is that something is going on, and it's not right beyond your peripheral vision — it's staring you so hard in the face that it's about to knock your eyes out, except I don't know what it is. But you know what it is. You know exactly what it is. What is it? (*Rosannah doesn't respond.*) How come you're not getting married?
ROSANNAH. What?
HENRY HARRY. What happened? You get a telegram informing you that your fiancé was wanted for murder in Nevada, or that he was already married to seven other women in seven other states — or that he used to be a woman or what?
ROSANNAH. No. No. Nothing like that.
HENRY HARRY. Then what?
ROSANNAH. I just . . . I was just . . .
HENRY HARRY. What?
ROSANNAH. (*Completely exasperated.*) Look! (*Beat.*) Listen! (*Beat.*) I am not standing here for one. If you could understand that simple fact, then you could perhaps see I am in no position to say why I didn't go through with the wedding.
HENRY HARRY. You are not standing here?
ROSANNAH. No. I am not.
HENRY HARRY. You are just not in a position at this time to say why you didn't go through with the wedding, because you are not *standing* here.
ROSANNAH. Yes.
HENRY HARRY. You're not *here*?

ROSANNAH. No . . . actually, no.

HENRY HARRY. (*Furious.*) You're just not here?! (*Rosannah refuses to answer. Henry Harry waits, but ascertains he will get no response.*) Ok. Alright. That's alright. That's fine. I don't care if you're here or not. You seem to be here to me, but — you know — whatever. (*He walks away, pauses, and turns.*) Just tell me one thing. (*Rosannah looks up.*) Just tell me — I mean you don't have to *be here* to tell me this — Just tell me from — wherever you are — ok? Tell me what happened.

ROSANNAH. What do you mean?

HENRY HARRY. I mean, you know, *what* happened. You arrived here in a wedding gown, so I assume you were fairly *close* to getting married — on the verge. So, just tell me what happened — how you went from being on the verge — to my door. (*Rosannah glares at him.*) I'm not asking for anything complicated. I don't need to know *why* you left or any of that — I just want to know *how* — you know? How you left. (*Guessing.*) You stood up and said, "I've changed my mind? I need time to think? I — "

ROSANNAH. No!

HENRY HARRY. No?

ROSANNAH. No, I didn't stand up and say anything.

HENRY HARRY. Ok. So, what'd you *do*?

ROSANNAH. (*After a pause.*) I had a problem with my feet.

HENRY HARRY. Your feet?

ROSANNAH. Yes. My feet would not move forward. I was standing in the back of the church and my feet would not move.

HENRY HARRY. You mean like you had a cramp or something?

ROSANNAH. No. Not like that. More like I was frozen. I felt like some frozen bird — like I was an animal of flight, but I was frozen — encased in ice. But I could see things and hear things all around me. (*She stops.*) Still I was encased in ice.

HENRY HARRY. Unhunh. . . . (*He waits, but Rosannah nods as if she's done.*) Yeah . . . but um . . . what did you do . . . I mean *exactly* what did you do? I'm just trying to get a sort of picture. I mean, exactly what did you do — with this ice and foot problem?

ROSANNAH. I just . . . I kept looking at the back of his head. That's all. He was up at the altar so I could see the back of his head. He wears his hair very short so it's very soft back there. And my heart went out to him. I mean my heart opened and something inside me wanted to rush out to him — something was fluttering in me — desperate to reach him, but I was frozen and not moving. (*She looks at Henry Harry.*) I could not move. That's all.
HENRY HARRY. That's all?
ROSANNAH. Yes. (*She sits down. She is done. She has explained everything. Henry Harry waits for a few seconds.*)
HENRY HARRY. Well — you must've moved. You're here.
ROSANNAH. Your heart can break you know? It's a real thing. It cracks and splits, and all this warm fluid comes out and, you can't move or speak or think because your veins are filled with it. (*She is almost immobile.*) I just stood there, looking at him, but I saw him differently.
HENRY HARRY. Differently than what?
ROSANNAH. Than I'd ever seen him before.
HENRY HARRY. How'd you see him?
ROSANNAH. Disconnected. Hovering. Alone — lonely. Just like me. Just like me, but I was awake, and he was asleep. Shhh. That was the difference. He was asleep. I felt I had to whisper. I felt like pain and loneliness — you know — LIFE — had put him to sleep forever, so we had to be very careful and whisper, because if he woke up, he'd wake up screaming, like me! Shhh, screaming! And I looked all over the church, at all those people, sound asleep, dead asleep. Asleep forever and ever, because everyone, if they woke up would wake up screaming! No! No one wants to wake up here. Shhh. This is a quiet place. This is a place where people are trying to sleep. People are trying to get some rest here — in this life. Be quiet. If they wake, they'll all wake screaming and I thought — WAKE UP ALL YOU TRAITORS! DON'T LEAVE ME ALONE! — But I whispered because my heart went out to them. My heart hurt, so I whispered and it was too much. Something was exploding out of me and all the while I was whispering. I knew I was in trouble. I thought I am going to be sick. Right here. Right now. I will be sick. So I just took four or five steps backwards out of the church — into the air,

but it was so hot and I was so dizzy, I went to my car — just to sit down, and then I thought I'll just drive it around the parking lot — just so some fresh air will blow on me. And once I started driving I couldn't stop. I was just blasting ahead. Don't crash! Don't crash! Don't crash into space . . . and then my car died. And now . . . I'm here. (*Henry Harry is dead silent. He takes all this in.*)

HENRY HARRY. I see.

ROSANNAH. That's how I left.

HENRY HARRY. Yeah . . . ok . . . yeah. (*Beat.*) You were in a state.

ROSANNAH. What?

HENRY HARRY. You were in the church in some kind of state.

ROSANNAH. (*Without rancor.*) I was not in a state.

HENRY HARRY. You were screaming. You were sick. You were in trouble.

ROSANNAH. No. I just walked backwards. I didn't make a sound. I just walked backwards until I was out the door, until I was in my car, and then I started driving — just for air.

HENRY HARRY. You said you were in trouble.

ROSANNAH. I was very quiet.

HENRY HARRY. Ok. Alright. You were very quiet.

ROSANNAH. Yes.

HENRY HARRY. You just quietly withdrew?

ROSANNAH. Yes.

HENRY HARRY. And you didn't say anything?

ROSANNAH. When?

HENRY HARRY. When you left. You didn't say, "Just a minute. I need some air."?

ROSANNAH. Oh. No. No, I didn't.

HENRY HARRY. You just withdrew.

ROSANNAH. Quietly.

HENRY HARRY. And everyone was still in the church?

ROSANNAH. In the church?

HENRY HARRY. Just sitting there. You didn't disturb anyone.

ROSANNAH. No. Not a soul. No one even noticed me go.

HENRY HARRY. And he was up at the altar — your fiancé — just standing there. I mean, that's how you left things?

32

ROSANNAH. Yes.

HENRY HARRY. And you haven't called him since?

ROSANNAH. Called him?

HENRY HARRY. Yes. I mean to let him know where you are — so he wouldn't worry.

ROSANNAH. Oh. No. No, I have not. No.

HENRY HARRY. But don't you think — I mean considering the circumstances of your departure — didn't you ever think of calling him?

ROSANNAH. What for?

HENRY HARRY. Well, think this through a minute. You just left a bunch of people in a church, waiting for you to walk up the aisle.

ROSANNAH. I had to get out of there.

HENRY HARRY. Ok. Fine. That's alright, but don't you think they are concerned? Don't you think he, specifically, is very concerned?

ROSANNAH. I don't know.

HENRY HARRY. You don't *know?*

ROSANNAH. No. I don't know what concerns other people.

HENRY HARRY. You don't know what concerns other people?

ROSANNAH. No.

HENRY HARRY. Well, if you were in the church, in a wedding gown, and you just disappeared, I can tell you —

ROSANNAH. (*Cutting him off.*) Look. Frankly, you can't tell me anything. You don't have any more idea what Bronco thinks about than *I* do.

HENRY HARRY. *Bronco?*

ROSANNAH. That's his nickname.

HENRY HARRY. *BRON CO?*

ROSANNAH. He's from Texas.

HENRY HARRY. What's his real name?

ROSANNAH. Walpole.

HENRY HARRY. *WALL POLE?*! (*Rosannah glares at him.*) WALL POLE what?

ROSANNAH. Walpole Weatherworth.

HENRY HARRY. You almost became Mrs. Walpole "Bronco" Weatherworth?

33

ROSANNAH. Oh for Pete's sake. (*Henry Harry bursts out laughing. He can't stop for some time. Rosannah holds back for a while, but his laughter is so delighted and contagious that soon she is laughing too. Finally Henry Harry pulls it together.*)

HENRY HARRY. Whew! (*Rosannah continues to giggle but with an edge. then, slowly, her laughter dissolves into embarrassed tears. Henry Harry notices, but keeps his distance. After a pause.*) Um. . . . Rosannah.

ROSANNAH. I've messed up. I've messed up real bad.

HENRY HARRY. I'm sure whatever happened. I'm sure you can—

ROSANNAH. I'm a weak person. I'm a very weak person. (*Henry Harry is troubled. Slowly he moves forward and sits down next to her. With difficulty, he finally puts his arm around her. She responds, sinking into him. Then, gently, he kisses her hair, her ears, her eyes—anywhere. She doesn't quite let him kiss her mouth. Suddenly she stands up confused, almost frightened.*) What are you doing?

HENRY HARRY. I'm kissing your ears.

ROSANNAH. Why?

HENRY HARRY. I don't know. (*He gets up awkwardly.*) I'm sorry. (*Beat.*) Are you alright?

ROSANNAH. Yes.

HENRY HARRY. Ok. Good. Good. I'm really sorry. I really didn't mean to kiss your ears. It just happened.

ROSANNAH. It's ok.

HENRY HARRY. I'm just—I'm a very vulnerable person to certain things.

ROSANNAH. I'm sorry. I mean it's ok.

HENRY HARRY. You were just . . . you were upset. It was an impulsive act on my part.

ROSANNAH. I know . . . I know.

HENRY HARRY. It happened before I was aware. It was just as much of a surprise to me as to you.

ROSANNAH. I understand.

HENRY HARRY. I was just sitting next to you, close to you—(*Suddenly terrified.*) Boyohboyohboyohboy-ohboyohboy.

ROSANNAH. What is it?

HENRY HARRY. Well—first of all—what am I doing?—

34

I mean who am I? — Who do I think I am? — What do I think I'm doing?

ROSANNAH. What are you talking about?

HENRY HARRY. Me! Me! Jesus! (*He runs to the sink and gets a small mirror and looks at himself.*)

ROSANNAH. What are you doing?

HENRY HARRY. I'm looking at myself. I'm taking a good look. (*He takes a good look. Then he brings the mirror over to Rosannah, and angles it at his face.*) Look!

ROSANNAH. I don't have to look in that mirror to see you.

HENRY HARRY. Oh. Yes. Well — (*Pointing to his face.*) look at this person! (*Rosannah looks.*) What do you see?

ROSANNAH. Well . . . I . . .

HENRY HARRY. You see an unsocialized person! You see someone who has lost certain elements of socialization. I'm not socialized anymore.

ROSANNAH. Yes you are.

HENRY HARRY. I'm not! I'm not!

ROSANNAH. Well, really you are. You made me soup.

HENRY HARRY. I also cooked your shoes and kissed your ears. That is not socialized behavior.

ROSANNAH. Well, nobody's perfect.

HENRY HARRY. Socialized behavior is when you offer someone a kleenex if they're upset. Do you want a kleenex?

ROSANNAH. No . . . actually, I used your shirt.

HENRY HARRY. Oh.

ROSANNAH. I'm not very socialized either.

HENRY HARRY. Oh, well, that's ok. That's alright . . . (*Settling down.*) I just gave myself a scare.

ROSANNAH. Oh.

HENRY HARRY. I have been essentially alone for a while.

ROSANNAH. Oh.

HENRY HARRY. A long while.

ROSANNAH. I see.

HENRY HARRY. Because the thing about people, well, you never know how they're going to affect you.

ROSANNAH. No. I guess you don't.

HENRY HARRY. They're the wild cards, as far as I'm concerned.

ROSANNAH. Oh.

35

HENRY HARRY. You can't control anything in your life when you have people running around in it.

ROSANNAH. No. You can't.

HENRY HARRY. So, I just steer clear of them. I have to. I have no choice. It's the only way I can keep a handle on things. Otherwise I wake up one morning and I don't know what I'm going to do next.

ROSANNAH. That's what my life is like too. That's why I fear I am not the one in the driver's seat. Because I never know what I will do next. From this moment to the next I don't know.

HENRY HARRY. (*Suddenly turning on her.*) Ha! Well, yeah! That's for sure!

ROSANNAH. What do you mean?

HENRY HARRY. Well . . . you're here. I mean when you think about it, it's pretty tough to figure how someone can be at a wedding, and not just any wedding, but *their own* wedding, in Arizona, and then — BAM — be on the highway, and then after driving for days and days on end, just — by chance — taking arbitrarily one turn after the next — end up at my door.

ROSANNAH. I'm sorry.

HENRY HARRY. I'm not asking you to apologize. It just seems *amazing* to me that you didn't go to some other place. I mean why didn't you go south for example.

ROSANNAH. *South?*

HENRY HARRY. If you'd gone south, you could still be driving. If you'd played your cards right you could have gone all the way down to Tierra del Fuego.

ROSANNAH. I didn't *want* to go to Tierra del Fuego.

HENRY HARRY. Well, why did you want to come here?

ROSANNAH. I didn't want to. I told you already. I *just came.*

HENRY HARRY. Nobody just comes here. Nobody!

ROSANNAH. Why are you attacking me?

HENRY HARRY. Who said I was attacking you?

ROSANNAH. I said.

HENRY HARRY. I'm not attacking you. I'm simply pointing out that nobody just happens to . . . to —

ROSANNAH. (*Interrupting.*) Kiss a total stranger's ears.

HENRY HARRY. What?!
ROSANNAH. It's the same thing. We both just had impulses.
HENRY HARRY. Impulses! Impulses! You drove three thousand miles on an impulse!?
ROSANNAH. I got in my car on an impulse. I don't remember the rest.
HENRY HARRY. Listen! You did a *gigantic, unbelievable* thing! I did a small —
ROSANNAH. SMALL! SMALL! Kissing somebody is not small! It's a *hugely* not small thing to do. It's *intimate! (Rosannah suddenly stops. She stands, out of breath. Her body seems almost to be moving towards Henry Harry. Yet she stays still. He makes a step towards her, and then backs off abruptly.)*
HENRY HARRY. WOA! *(Beat.)* Woa! Woa! Hold on! There is something you gotta understand. Something I think we gotta get straight. I have worked very hard to have this . . . this *life* MY LIFE! I work — I cook — I come here and I live . . . I try to live . . . I've been trying to kind of *live.* That's all. It takes a certain amount of effort.
ROSANNAH. Effort?
HENRY HARRY. Yes. Just to live — it takes a certain amount of effort. In fact, it takes *all* my effort just to live and not to . . . to . . . *(With violence.)* tear everything to shreds. *(Calming down.)* And I do alright. I have been, for quite some time, doing alright . . . I *thought* I was doing alright. And *now, now* you come along and it's like I am just holding onto the deck, just holding on, but underneath, right directly underneath, there is a current about to tear me right the hell away from whatever it is, whatever little safe harbor I've managed to latch onto. I can feel it. I mean I'm in with the sharks now and I mean — Jesus Christ — what happened to you? WHO ARE YOU? WHY ARE YOU HERE? IN MY LIFE?
ROSANNAH. It's not my fault.
HENRY HARRY. I'm not saying it's your fault.
ROSANNAH. You *are!* And it's *not!* I told you already I'd go to a hotel or something. I *want* to go to a hotel or something.
HENRY HARRY. There are no "hotels or something" around here. That's exactly why I'm *here.* That's the *whole point.*

ROSANNAH. Well, I'm sorry I'm intruding. I really truly am. I understand you've got your life and all. I've got mine too. I am also trying very hard not to tear everything to shreds! Did that ever occur to you? That I am making a huge effort too? But what can I do? Here? Now? (*Suddenly turning around.*) Ok. I know. (*She takes a chair and places it in a corner, facing the wall.*) I'll just sit over here. (*She sits.*)
HENRY HARRY. What are you doing?
ROSANNAH. I'm using up as little of your — privacy — as I can.
HENRY HARRY. That's very funny.
ROSANNAH. I'm not trying to be funny.
HENRY HARRY. You're just going to sit over in that corner.
ROSANNAH. Until the storm's over.
HENRY HARRY. Until the storm's over! The storm might not be over till next July!
ROSANNAH. I don't give a hoot when the storm's over. I'm just going to sit here.
HENRY HARRY. And I'm supposed to just go about my business while you just sit there — in that chair — in that corner.
ROSANNAH. Look — you know — you are not the only person in the world who would prefer at this particular time to be left alone.
HENRY HARRY. Oh! Oh! Excuse me! I get it! You blast into my home, my *sanctuary*, from Arizona, and then inform me that you'd like to be left alone.
ROSANNAH. (*Suddenly standing.*) At least I am trying to be polite, but *yes*, I would like to be alone. *Yes*, I wish you weren't here. Yes! As a matter of fact, I wish I'd come here on one of the weeks when you were on that oil rig. That's what I wish. Ok? How do you think it feels to wake up in Alaska, in some barn or whatever this is, with an angry hostile stranger —
HENRY HARRY. I made you a cauldron of soup!
ROSANNAH. YOU COOKED MY SHOES! (*Beat.*) And you've made it very clear that you don't want me here.
HENRY HARRY. I don't want anybody here.
ROSANNAH. Well, I don't want to be here either. You think I *want* to be here? I don't. I wanted to die. That's what I

wanted. I wanted to die, but instead I am falling backwards — out of the church — I am flying forward into space. Then somehow, through no will of my own, I am driving. Driving and driving — all the time wishing my car would just evaporate on the road, wishing I would just fly out, unleashed like some wild released coil — out and out until I am nothing, dust, air — I thought this might happen and I welcomed it. But instead, I am thrown into this freezing storm — this white out, and I suddenly realize I'm going to die and I want to LIVE! Who is in charge of these decisions? I say, *not me!* So I get out of the car and save myself and the fact is, I don't *like* it. I don't. Life — Death. It's all one big tragedy. Someone can love you . . . can touch your soul — that's what they can do — *touch your soul,* and then — BAM — something happens and they can't even remember you. They look at you and can't quite remember you — after they've *touched your soul.* After they've made an indentation on your *soul.* After they've dug into you so deep that they are part of you, part of every cell, part of your skin, and under your skin, so that digging them out leaves you full of gorged places, routed out holes, disfigured, ruined, and alone. (*She turns around and faces away. Henry Harry waits, but she doesn't continue.*)

HENRY HARRY. What are we talking about? (*There is no reply.*) I can see we're talking about something and I want to know *what?*

ROSANNAH. Nothing. We're not talking about anything.

HENRY HARRY. Oh yes we are. We are definitely talking about *some*thing.

ROSANNAH. Well, whatever it was, we're not talking about it anymore.

HENRY HARRY. Yes we are. We're still talking about it, and I want to know what it is. What is it? Did your husband/fiancé/Bronco/Walpole — whoever the hell he is — did he . . . *say* something?

ROSANNAH. What?

HENRY HARRY. Did he do something — not do something? What?

ROSANNAH. No. This has nothing to do with him.

HENRY HARRY. Then what does it have to do with?

ROSANNAH. I don't know. Nothing. Not you! That's for sure! Not you!

HENRY HARRY. Not me! Not me! Let me tell you something. I am all screwed up now — Look at me! LOOK AT ME! I am standing here all screwed up, ok? And I wasn't like this till you came through that door. Before you came, I was becoming a gray man. That's all I wanted to become — a gray man — that's all I have wanted. And now I am standing here. My heart is pounding. I'm sweating. Just five minutes ago I was kissing your ears. And I don't know what's going to happen next. I don't know. The truth is, that half my mental energy at this particular time is fixed on the fact that for reasons I can't fathom I want to kiss you more, ok? And, at the same time — in the very same moment, the other half is fixed on the fact that for other *very clear* reasons, I don't want to kiss you more. Are you beginning to see where I am? I am in a state! I am standing here about to *explode* — so don't tell me this has nothing to do with *me*. This has to do with me, and don't tell me this has nothing to do with Walpole/Bronco. Whatever happened, he's affected. I AM SURE he's affected, just as I am affected and you are affected. Because *you* are traveling from here to kingdom come with some wild kind of energy in you and flinging it out at everything that gets in your path, and I am, right at this moment, in your path, and I want to know what's hitting me. I want to know what the hell we're talking about, and I want to know NOW.

ROSANNAH. (*After a pause.*) I'm sorry I've upset you.

HENRY HARRY. You're sorry you've upset me?

ROSANNAH. I just want to be left alone.

HENRY HARRY. That's too bad.

ROSANNAH. What's that supposed to mean?

HENRY HARRY. That means it's too bad that's what you want 'cause you can't have it. I'm here. See me! You're not alone.

ROSANNAH. I can see that.

HENRY HARRY. So what do we do now?

ROSANNAH. About what?

HENRY HARRY. About the fact that we're both here?

ROSANNAH. Nothing. We don't do anything.

HENRY HARRY. I disagree. I say you tell me what you

were talking about back there. I say you clue me in and you clue me in now.

ROSANNAH. Or what?! You beat me up! You lock me out! You throw me into the snowstorm — don't feed me or clothe me or let me sleep here? What? What? (*Suddenly physically attacking him with her fists.*) You listen to me! You can't hurt me! You can't hurt me! Go ahead! Come on!

HENRY HARRY. (*Trying to fend her off.*) Stop it!

ROSANNAH. Go ahead! Beat me up! Tear me to shreds! Go ahead! I don't care! I don't care! You can't hurt me! You could *kill* me and you wouldn't hurt me. (*She is throwing her fists at him with serious intent. He fends her off, grabbing both arms and holding her. Then, suddenly, he kisses her violently and passionately. He lets go of her fists and she puts her arms around him. Suddenly he pulls away, very distraught.*)

HENRY HARRY. I'm kissing your mouth. Now I'm kissing your mouth. I wanted to do it. I did it. (*Backing away.*) Jesus Christ! What the hell am I doing? Where the hell am I going? I was living here alone, minding my own business and now, suddenly, I'm going somewhere. Now I'm traveling. Where? I don't know. And I'll tell you another thing. Even after I get there I won't know where I am. Well, no thanks — I rode that roller coaster already. *You* stay away from me!

ROSANNAH. Me?

HENRY HARRY. Yes.

ROSANNAH. I haven't *done* anything.

HENRY HARRY. You came in here with those shoes!

ROSANNAH. What?

HENRY HARRY. You came in here, in the middle of the night, freezing to death, wearing paper shoes . . . little, tiny, paper . . . (*Turning on her fiercely.*) you don't know what life is like for me. You don't begin to know. I have tried always to steer clear of whatever this stuff is — all this — stuff, but I cannot. It finds me. It eats me up. It eats me up and never fully destroys me. No. It leaves shreds of me, just shreds — to come back for later. I was a kid — you know — just hanging out — and I met this girl, Nora, and she got knocked up — I mean by me. I'm not trying to remove myself, even if I felt removed at the time. Even if I felt like I was living in the freezer. So I went to live with her, take care of

41

her. I never really loved her, but she got sick and needed help and since I had got her in this mess — I don't know — I just went. And then she had this little baby. We called her Annabelle. And it was like — I just woke up forever. I loved her. From just the minute she was born. That's what love is — something that just overcomes you and you can't stop it. So I stayed. And when Annabelle got to be about three, she had all these dolls she played with. And these dolls had little tiny clothing and even little rings and bracelets — so sometimes you might look on the floor and find some tiny little silver thing — looks like it's made out of tinfoil, but you *never, never* threw those things away because they belonged to Annabelle — I mean to one of her little dolls. And for her, these things were *precious*. Even their little shoes were precious. I was constantly finding these little doll shoes all over the house and saving them for her, and she would be so happy to see that long lost shoe and put it on her little doll's foot. What I'm saying is — I could make her happy that way, just by finding a tiny little shoe . . . so some nights, after she was asleep, I would get down on my hands and knees and just scour the living room floor where she played, just in hopes that I would find a little shoe or something — and the next day make her happy — but then, one time, I was sweeping up and not really paying attention, and I think out of the corner of my eye, I saw this little blue thing go into the dustpan — you know — but my mind was preoccupied and *anyway,* you can't just be alert every single minute, so I just threw it in the trash, and the very next morning, the *very next,* she comes downstairs with this barefoot doll, looking for a little blue shoe — she's lost one of her shoes, and I *knew* immediately, but I mean you can't just go through the garbage every time a little tiny blue shoe gets lost, so I lied — I mean it wasn't really lying because I didn't know for sure that that was the thing I'd thrown away, but it was lying because I did know — and *now* — all the time I think about that lie — all the time. And some days I imagine myself going through the garbage and finding that shoe and washing it and giving it to her and she's so very happy, so very happy — so when you left those shoes out — what could I do? You see my situation? They were not *nothing*. They were not nothing

lying there. They were *something*. I had to do something with them. I had no choice. I just put them under the broiler and put it on high heat. Here! (*He runs to the broiler and takes out the broiler pan, with the burnt shoes. He brings it over to Rosannah.*) There!
ROSANNAH. Oh . . . (*She examines the black lumps sadly.*)
HENRY HARRY. I cooked them on purpose.
ROSANNAH. Oh.
HENRY HARRY. I destroyed them. I purposefully, willfully, destroyed them.
ROSANNAH. Oh.
HENRY HARRY. I don't know what happened to me. I just . . . I lost control or something. I can't remember. The main thing was I just wanted them out of my sight. I didn't want to—I couldn't . . . could not look at them.
ROSANNAH. (*Examining them closely.*) You really, really cooked them.
HENRY HARRY. Yes. I'm sorry.
ROSANNAH. (*With difficulty.*) They're just shoes.
HENRY HARRY. They were valuable shoes.
ROSANNAH. No. The truth is, I got them on sale.
HENRY HARRY. Oh.
ROSANNAH. They were reduced considerably.
HENRY HARRY. Oh.
ROSANNAH. They were for my wedding.
HENRY HARRY. I know.
ROSANNAH. (*Turning the shoes over. She can't quite yet believe the shoes' fate.*) The lace edges are pretty well . . . (*Pulling off a black filament.*) I mean, looking at them now, it would be hard to reconstruct that they ever had lace edges.
HENRY HARRY. I didn't know what I was doing. (*Rosannah holds the shoes to her and begins to cry.*) Oh no. (*Beat.*) Oh no.
ROSANNAH. No. I'm fine. I get like this. It's just nerves.
HENRY HARRY. You're crying.
ROSANNAH. No. I'm not really. This is not really crying.
HENRY HARRY. It is too really crying.
ROSANNAH. No it's not. It's just a tremor. Just a little tremor. I just get these little tremors.

43

HENRY HARRY. Would you like something? Would you like a glass of water?

ROSANNAH. No. No.

HENRY HARRY. It wasn't personal. It wasn't about you.

ROSANNAH. I understand.

HENRY HARRY. I just . . . I . . .

ROSANNAH. Where's Annabelle now?

HENRY HARRY. She had a . . . there was an accident.

ROSANNAH. What kind of accident?

HENRY HARRY. She fell . . . she took a bad fall.

ROSANNAH. What happened?

HENRY HARRY. She took a very bad fall. She was up on the kitchen counter, next to the sink. Nora had just washed her hair, and she was lying there, like always, except Nora had forgotten to get a towel, and she went to the cupboard, just a couple of steps away, and I came in the back door, sort of at the other end of the room and I guess it was slippery and wet and soapy up there, but Annabelle just reached out, just stretched out her arms to me. I mean she was happy to see me, and then she kind of turned sideways and just slid off.

ROSANNAH. She just slid off?

HENRY HARRY. Yes.

ROSANNAH. Oh no.

HENRY HARRY. I ran up to catch her. I ran straight up there. I was almost there when she hit the floor.

ROSANNAH. Oh.

HENRY HARRY. And there was a small truck there, a toy truck, and this part of her head, this one little part of her head hit the edge of the truck, I mean, evidently, there's this one little corner of your head where if you were to fall and hit it on a little toy truck . . . so.

ROSANNAH. Oh no.

HENRY HARRY. Yeah. Well . . .

ROSANNAH. Oh no.

HENRY HARRY. It was, you know, it was . . . I mean there were possibilities of saving her. I've thought this through a lot. And there were actually three possibilities.

ROSANNAH. What possibilities?

HENRY HARRY. Well. One is if Nora had not forgotten the towel — but you cannot really *blame* Nora for that. Peo-

44

ple often forget little things like towels. And then, two, is if Annabelle had not stretched out her arms and rolled sideways, but she was a small child. I mean balance is something even an adult occasionally underestimates. And then, three, and the last and final hope to save her, is if I had caught her.

ROSANNAH. It wasn't your fault!

HENRY HARRY. You weren't there. You cannot imagine how close.

ROSANNAH. But it was *not* your fault!

HENRY HARRY. YOU CANNOT IMAGINE HOW CLOSE! (*Abruptly.*) Why aren't you getting married? Hmmm? I would really like to know why you aren't getting married? I would. I would really like you to tell me exactly why you took five steps backwards and found yourself outside the church, and then the parking lot, and then the car and now here! Tell me! (*Rosannah watches this abrupt change with concern and fear. Slowly she moves towards him, to touch him.*) No! Don't touch me! Don't you come near me.

ROSANNAH. I won't hurt you.

HENRY HARRY. You won't *hurt* me? You think you won't *hurt* me? Look! Look! Look at this! (*Pointing to his arm.*) Look! (*Rosannah looks.*) And here! (*His wrist.*) I have scars all over my body. Dozens and dozens. (*Pointing to the flat center palm of his left hand.*) This one I got just from touching the top of her head. This one . . . this one . . . (*Unbuttoning his shirt and exposing his chest.*) was when she fell asleep. Her cheek was right here. (*He points to a spot on his chest.*) Here — (*Now touching the outer corner of his eye.*) from when she kissed me. I have hundreds of them. Hundreds and hundreds! Like stars all over my body. (*Henry Harry collapses in a corner. Rosannah moves over to him slowly, to help him, but she cannot touch him. Finally she backs away to a chair. She sits down and addresses him. She is in a state of great tension.*)

ROSANNAH. Did you ever think that one time, a long time ago, when you were a little child, you were visited by extraterrestrials? They say that when you are visited by an extraterrestrial — after the visit, the extraterrestrial puts this spell on you so you cannot remember the encounter at all, and you wake up only with this sad kind of longing for something, but you don't know what. And you carry that sad

45

longing with you all the rest of your life. And they say that if, by chance, you get hypnotized, then you reveal the encounter, under hypnosis and when you wake up, you remember it, and then, it is no longer a sad longing, but a real thing, which you know about, and even if people think you're crazy, talking ali the time about your extraterrestrial encounter, that's ok, because in your heart you know what it was that had been locked up for so long and you are greatly relieved. (*Beat.*) I have often wondered what it would feel like to be greatly relieved. (*She rises and approaches Henry Harry standing closer, but still unable to touch him.*) I am not a very healthy person as I have said. I am, at this point in my life, relying on the long shot. I have really truly reached a point where I almost have expectations that an extraterrestrial will come to me. That I will see him and feel connected to him — right away, and he will say, Yes! It was me! It was me who touched you. And I won't care if he is very small or if he is milky white. I won't care at all, if I just know he is the one. (*Beat.*) If I just know he is the one.

HENRY HARRY. No. I don't believe in extraterrestrials. I can't.

ROSANNAH. Can't?

HENRY HARRY. Someone who just shows up at your door from outer space — I doubt it.

ROSANNAH. But the possibility —

HENRY HARRY. (*Rising.*) The possibility? The *possibility*? Do you want to know how Annabelle *really* died? Do you? (*Rosannah looks up startled. Suddenly exploding.*) I loved her. That's all. If I had not loved her so much she never would have stretched out her arms and turned to me.

ROSANNAH. (*In a barely controlled whispered anger.*) What are you trying to do? Wipe her out? Take her life away from her? Don't you understand! She *had* something. She was loved. If no one had loved her she would have been . . . (*She trails off.*)

HENRY HARRY. What?

ROSANNAH. (*With difficulty.*) Indistinguishable.

HENRY HARRY. What do you mean?

ROSANNAH. I mean that's not being alive. Just being obliterated like that. Turned into nothing? Just waking up one morning and looking at a chair, and it's not a chair anymore. It's nothing. Something that might attack you. Nothing. Nothing that means anything to you. Nothing. (*She grabs a chair and crashes it to the ground, smashing it, and letting out a horrible growl.*) Or looking at your own daughter and she's nothing. No one — a burden you have shucked off. Look at me! Look at me! (*She waits for him to really look.*) There was a time in my life when I was bound for glory. Every day I was bound for glory. I had expectations. Do you understand me? I was connected to this earth. I was alive! And now I am just hovering, hovering, hovering! And I can't stand it. I can't. I want to land. I want to come in for a landing.

HENRY HARRY. You're not hovering. You're here!

ROSANNAH. No I'm not! I'm not! (*Almost shivering and in a state of great tension.*) I was at my wedding, in the vestry, getting ready to go in, and there he was. I didn't even know he was coming. Surprise! And I said, "Daddy!", and he looked around like he thought someone else had come in, and I said, "Daddy! It's me. Rosannah." And he smiled and looked right into my face, right into it, and said, "It's so nice to meet you, Rosannah. I do believe you're the prettiest little girl I've ever seen." His eyes looked right into mine and he saw nothing. Bam! Blink! And all the bright places I had lived in him went dark. Just like that. I just wanted to help him. Bang the floodlights on! So I hit him. I knocked him right against the wall. I punched him with my fists. His head started bleeding, but that didn't stop me. I wanted to hurt him. I wanted to kill him.

HENRY HARRY. But it wasn't his fault!

ROSANNAH. I don't care. He's in my skin and under my skin. He is in every cell. He is part of me. He's in my DNA, and I could feel him being gouged out. I could feel myself being ripped to shreds. I could feel the light in every cell in my body being spit out. I could feel myself being disconnected, cut loose, and hurtled into space, and I thought I have to have someone. If I don't have someone, I will die — I will fly wild and crash. I need someone. Is that too much to ask for? One person out there who is awake and *sees* you? One person who connects you to this earth? One person who lets you know — Yes! He is the one. He is the one!

47

HENRY HARRY. (*Moving forward to hold her.*) Rosannah.

ROSANNAH. No. You just want to wipe everyone out.

HENRY HARRY. (*Overlapping.*) No I don't.

ROSANNAH. Well, you don't have to wipe *me* out, because I'm not here.

HENRY HARRY. You *are* here. Please—

ROSANNAH. (*Getting away from him.*) Leave me alone.

HENRY HARRY. I won't leave you alone. (*Holding her.*) Listen to me. You're right here. With me. I can feel you.

ROSANNAH. This has nothing to do with you. Nothing. It's just me. It's—

HENRY HARRY. Just you? Just you! There is no *just you!*

ROSANNAH. Yes. There is! I am—I am—I am—

HENRY HARRY. (*Taking physical control of her, and holding her face.*) You are the prettiest girl I have ever seen. (*Rosannah is stilled. His hand traveling down to her heart.*) Your heart is beating very fast.

ROSANNAH. No, it's not.

HENRY HARRY. I feel it.

ROSANNAH. No you don't.

HENRY HARRY. You can feel it too. (*Rosannah suddenly throws him off and flies as far away from him as she can get. He chases after her.*)

ROSANNAH. I can't. No! Let me go! I'm not here. I'm in danger. I'm in great danger.

HENRY HARRY. (*Catching her and trying to hold her.*) No. I've got you. You're here. (*Rosannah shoves him and runs wildly and irrationally up to the counter, trying to escape. She flies up, hits the wall, and as she cries out her lines, loses her balance and flies backwards into the air.*)

ROSANNAH. No. I'll crash! I'll crash! I'll crash! I'll crash! I'll crash! (*She screams, and just as it looks as if she will hurtle to the ground, Henry Harry makes a dive and catches her in his arms.*)

HENRY HARRY. I've got you! (*She is still terrorized, as he holds her close and the lights fade slowly to black.*)

# END OF PLAY

*N.B. If the physical nature of the actors or the set make it untruth-ful for Henry Harry to catch Rosannah in mid-flight, the ending can be achieved by Rosannah simply pushing away from Henry Harry on her line, "I'm in great danger.", stumbling and falling wildly to the floor, as he struggles to both catch her and get her to "see", on the last line, that he's got her.*

# PROPERTY LIST

Bed:
  2 blankets
  2 sheets
  pillow

U of Bed:
  Shirt (R's)
  Pants
  Booties

Chair L:
  Pretzels (on seat)
  Pants (H's – over back)
  Shirt (H's – over pants)

Counter:
  Bottom Shelf:
    Basin
    Plastic water jug
    Collander
  Middle Shelf:
    Bread on platter (2 slices)
    Butter, knife, on oval plate
    Copper pot & lid
    White bowl
  Counter L:
    Soup bowl
    Towels
  Sink:
    Plugged
    Towel on L. faucet
  Counter R:
    Silver can:
      Ladle
      2 soup spoons
      Wooden spoon
    Tea cannister w/tea bags
    Serving spoon
    2 blue mugs

Top Shelf:
    Mirror (R)
    4 books

Stove:
  Soup cauldron
  Tea
  Lid
  Burners
  Broiler pan:
      Ashes
      Shoes

Table:
  Whiskey

Chair:
  under table R.
  Rubber mallet
  Water pumped (Pops)
  Plaid blanket
  Empty pan of water

SCENE DESIGN
"BRILLIANT TRACES"

BED

STOVE  SINK & COUNTER

CHAIR

TABLE

CHAIR

DOOR

# NEW PLAYS

★ MOTHERHOOD OUT LOUD by Leslie Ayvazian, Brooke Berman, David Cale, Jessica Goldberg, Beth Henley, Lameece Issaq, Claire LaZebnik, Lisa Loomer, Michele Lowe, Marco Pennette, Theresa Rebeck, Luanne Rice, Annie Weisman and Cheryl L. West, conceived by Susan R. Rose and Joan Stein. When entrusting the subject of motherhood to such a dazzling collection of celebrated American writers, what results is a joyous, moving, hilarious, and altogether thrilling theatrical event. "Never fails to strike both the funny bone and the heart." –*BackStage.* "Packed with wisdom, laughter, and plenty of wry surprises." –*TheaterMania.* [1M, 3W] ISBN: 978-0-8222-2589-8

★ COCK by Mike Bartlett. When John takes a break from his boyfriend, he accidentally meets the girl of his dreams. Filled with guilt and indecision, he decides there is only one way to straighten this out. "[A] brilliant and blackly hilarious feat of provocation." –*Independent.* "A smart, prickly and rewarding view of sexual and emotional confusion." –*Evening Standard.* [3M, 1W] ISBN: 978-0-8222-2766-3

★ F. Scott Fitzgerald's THE GREAT GATSBY adapted for the stage by Simon Levy. Jay Gatsby, a self-made millionaire, passionately pursues the elusive Daisy Buchanan. Nick Carraway, a young newcomer to Long Island, is drawn into their world of obsession, greed and danger. "Levy's combination of narration, dialogue and action delivers most of what is best in the novel." –*Seattle Post-Intelligencer.* "A beautifully crafted interpretation of the 1925 novel which defined the Jazz Age." –*London Free Press.* [5M, 4W] ISBN: 978-0-8222-2727-4

★ LONELY, I'M NOT by Paul Weitz. At an age when most people are discovering what they want to do with their lives, Porter has been married and divorced, earned seven figures as a corporate "ninja," and had a nervous breakdown. It's been four years since he's had a job or a date, and he's decided to give life another shot. "Critic's pick!" –*NY Times.* "An enjoyable ride." –*NY Daily News.* [3M, 3W] ISBN: 978-0-8222-2734-2

★ ASUNCION by Jesse Eisenberg. Edgar and Vinny are not racist. In fact, Edgar maintains a blog condemning American imperialism, and Vinny is three-quarters into a Ph.D. in Black Studies. When Asuncion becomes their new roommate, the boys have a perfect opportunity to demonstrate how open-minded they truly are. "Mr. Eisenberg writes lively dialogue that strikes plenty of comic sparks." –*NY Times.* "An almost ridiculously enjoyable portrait of slacker trauma among would-be intellectuals." –*Newsday.* [2M, 2W] ISBN: 978-0-8222-2630-7

**DRAMATISTS PLAY SERVICE, INC.**
440 Park Avenue South, New York, NY 10016  212-683-8960  Fax 212-213-1539
*postmaster@dramatists.com*  www.dramatists.com

# NEW PLAYS

★ **THE PICTURE OF DORIAN GRAY by Roberto Aguirre-Sacasa, based on the novel by Oscar Wilde.** Preternaturally handsome Dorian Gray has his portrait painted by his college classmate Basil Hallwood. When their mutual friend Henry Wotton offers to include it in a show, Dorian makes a fateful wish—that his portrait should grow old instead of him—and strikes an unspeakable bargain with the devil. [5M, 2W] ISBN: 978-0-8222-2590-4

★ **THE LYONS by Nicky Silver.** As Ben Lyons lies dying, it becomes clear that he and his wife have been at war for many years, and his impending demise has brought no relief. When they're joined by their children all efforts at a sentimental goodbye to the dying patriarch are soon abandoned. "Hilariously frank, clear-sighted, compassionate and forgiving." –*NY Times.* "Mordant, dark and rich." –*Associated Press.* [3M, 3W] ISBN: 978-0-8222-2659-8

★ **STANDING ON CEREMONY by Mo Gaffney, Jordan Harrison, Moisés Kaufman, Neil LaBute, Wendy MacLeod, José Rivera, Paul Rudnick, and Doug Wright, conceived by Brian Shnipper.** Witty, warm and occasionally wacky, these plays are vows to the blessings of equality, the universal challenges of relationships and the often hilarious power of love. "CEREMONY puts a human face on a hot-button issue and delivers laughter and tears rather than propaganda." –*BackStage.* [3M, 3W] ISBN: 978-0-8222-2654-3

★ **ONE ARM by Moisés Kaufman, based on the short story and screenplay by Tennessee Williams.** Ollie joins the Navy and becomes the lightweight boxing champion of the Pacific Fleet. Soon after, he loses his arm in a car accident, and he turns to hustling to survive. "[A] fast, fierce, brutally beautiful stage adaptation." –*NY Magazine.* "A fascinatingly lurid, provocative and fatalistic piece of theater." –*Variety.* [7M, 1W] ISBN: 978-0-8222-2564-5

★ **AN ILIAD by Lisa Peterson and Denis O'Hare.** A modern-day retelling of Homer's classic. Poetry and humor, the ancient tale of the Trojan War and the modern world collide in this captivating theatrical experience. "Shocking, glorious, primal and deeply satisfying." –*Time Out NY.* "Explosive, altogether breathtaking." –*Chicago Sun-Times.* [1M] ISBN: 978-0-8222-2687-1

★ **THE COLUMNIST by David Auburn.** At the height of the Cold War, Joe Alsop is the nation's most influential journalist, beloved, feared and courted by the Washington world. But as the '60s dawn and America undergoes dizzying change, the intense political dramas Joe is embroiled in become deeply personal as well. "Intensely satisfying." –*Bloomberg News.* [5M, 2W] ISBN: 978-0-8222-2699-4

**DRAMATISTS PLAY SERVICE, INC.**
440 Park Avenue South, New York, NY 10016  212-683-8960  Fax 212-213-1539
postmaster@dramatists.com  www.dramatists.com

# NEW PLAYS

★ **BENGAL TIGER AT THE BAGHDAD ZOO by Rajiv Joseph.** The lives of two American Marines and an Iraqi translator are forever changed by an encounter with a quick-witted tiger who haunts the streets of war-torn Baghdad. "[A] boldly imagined, harrowing and surprisingly funny drama." –*NY Times.* "Tragic yet darkly comic and highly imaginative." –*CurtainUp.* [5M, 2W] ISBN: 978-0-8222-2565-2

★ **THE PITMEN PAINTERS by Lee Hall, inspired by a book by William Feaver.** Based on the triumphant true story, a group of British miners discover a new way to express themselves and unexpectedly become art-world sensations. "Excitingly ambiguous, in-the-moment theater." –*NY Times.* "Heartfelt, moving and deeply politicized." –*Chicago Tribune.* [5M, 2W] ISBN: 978-0-8222-2507-2

★ **RELATIVELY SPEAKING by Ethan Coen, Elaine May and Woody Allen.** In TALKING CURE, Ethan Coen uncovers the sort of insanity that can only come from family. Elaine May explores the hilarity of passing in GEORGE IS DEAD. In HONEYMOON MOTEL, Woody Allen invites you to the sort of wedding day you won't forget. "Firecracker funny." –*NY Times.* "A rollicking good time." –*New Yorker.* [8M, 7W] ISBN: 978-0-8222-2394-8

★ **SONS OF THE PROPHET by Stephen Karam.** If to live is to suffer, then Joseph Douaihy is more alive than most. With unexplained chronic pain and the fate of his reeling family on his shoulders, Joseph's health, sanity, and insurance premium are on the line. "Explosively funny." –*NY Times.* "At once deep, deft and beautifully made." –*New Yorker.* [5M, 3W] ISBN: 978-0-8222-2597-3

★ **THE MOUNTAINTOP by Katori Hall.** A gripping reimagination of events the night before the assassination of the civil rights leader Dr. Martin Luther King, Jr. "An ominous electricity crackles through the opening moments." –*NY Times.* "[A] thrilling, wild, provocative flight of magical realism." –*Associated Press.* "Crackles with theatricality and a humanity more moving than sainthood." –*NY Newsday.* [1M, 1W] ISBN: 978-0-8222-2603-1

★ **ALL NEW PEOPLE by Zach Braff.** Charlie is 35, heartbroken, and just wants some time away from the rest of the world. Long Beach Island seems to be the perfect escape until his solitude is interrupted by a motley parade of misfits who show up and change his plans. "Consistently and sometimes sensationally funny." –*NY Times.* "A morbidly funny play about the trendy new existential condition of being young, adorable, and miserable." –*Variety.* [2M, 2W] ISBN: 978-0-8222-2562-1

**DRAMATISTS PLAY SERVICE, INC.**
440 Park Avenue South, New York, NY 10016  212-683-8960  Fax 212-213-1539
postmaster@dramatists.com  www.dramatists.com

# NEW PLAYS

★ **CLYBOURNE PARK by Bruce Norris.** WINNER OF THE 2011 PULITZER PRIZE AND 2012 TONY AWARD. Act One takes place in 1959 as community leaders try to stop the sale of a home to a black family. Act Two is set in the same house in the present day as the now predominantly African-American neighborhood battles to hold its ground. "Vital, sharp-witted and ferociously smart." –*NY Times.* "A theatrical treasure…Indisputably, uproariously funny." –*Entertainment Weekly.* [4M, 3W] ISBN: 978-0-8222-2697-0

★ **WATER BY THE SPOONFUL by Quiara Alegría Hudes.** WINNER OF THE 2012 PULITZER PRIZE. A Puerto Rican veteran is surrounded by the North Philadelphia demons he tried to escape in the service. "This is a very funny, warm, and yes uplifting play." –*Hartford Courant.* "The play is a combination poem, prayer and app on how to cope in an age of uncertainty, speed and chaos." –*Variety.* [4M, 3W] ISBN: 978-0-8222-2716-8

★ **RED by John Logan.** WINNER OF THE 2010 TONY AWARD. Mark Rothko has just landed the biggest commission in the history of modern art. But when his young assistant, Ken, gains the confidence to challenge him, Rothko faces the agonizing possibility that his crowning achievement could also become his undoing. "Intense and exciting." –*NY Times.* "Smart, eloquent entertainment." –*New Yorker.* [2M] ISBN: 978-0-8222-2483-9

★ **VENUS IN FUR by David Ives.** Thomas, a beleaguered playwright/director, is desperate to find an actress to play Vanda, the female lead in his adaptation of the classic sadomasochistic tale *Venus in Fur.* "Ninety minutes of good, kinky fun." –*NY Times.* "A fast-paced journey into one man's entrapment by a clever, vengeful female." –*Associated Press.* [1M, 1W] ISBN: 978-0-8222-2603-1

★ **OTHER DESERT CITIES by Jon Robin Baitz.** Brooke returns home to Palm Springs after a six-year absence and announces that she is about to publish a memoir dredging up a pivotal and tragic event in the family's history—a wound they don't want reopened. "Leaves you feeling both moved and gratifyingly sated." –*NY Times.* "A genuine pleasure." –*NY Post.* [2M, 3W] ISBN: 978-0-8222-2605-5

★ **TRIBES by Nina Raine.** Billy was born deaf into a hearing family and adapts brilliantly to his family's unconventional ways, but it's not until he meets Sylvia, a young woman on the brink of deafness, that he finally understands what it means to be understood. "A smart, lively play." –*NY Times.* "[A] bright and boldly provocative drama." –*Associated Press.* [3M, 2W] ISBN: 978-0-8222-2751-9

**DRAMATISTS PLAY SERVICE, INC.**
440 Park Avenue South, New York, NY 10016  212-683-8960  Fax 212-213-1539
postmaster@dramatists.com  www.dramatists.com